# The Soviet Bloc Role In International Terrorism And Revolutionary Violence

# Contents

**The Soviet Bloc Role In International Terrorism And Revolutionary Violence** ............ ii

**Publishing Information** ............ iii

**AI-generated Bibliographic Keywords** ............ iii

**Publisher's Notes** ............ iii

**Abstracts** ............ iv
    TL;DR (one word) ............ iv
    Explain It To Me Like I'm Five Years Old ............ iv
    Synopsis ............ iv
    Scientific Style ............ v
    Action Items (Prospective) ............ v

**Viewpoints** ............ vii
    Three Most Important Takewawys for Present-Day Readers ............ vii
    Grounds for Dissent ............ vii
    Red Team Critique ............ ix
    MAGA Perspective ............ xi

# The Soviet Bloc Role In International Terrorism And Revolutionary Violence

Nimble Books LLC: The AI Lab for Book-Lovers

Fred Zimmerman, Editor

*Humans and AI making books richer, more diverse, and more surprising*

# Publishing Information

- (c) 2024 Nimble Books LLC
- ISBN: 978-1-60888-320-2

# AI-generated Bibliographic Keywords

the Soviet Bloc role in international terrorism; Soviet Bloc support for revolutionary violence; National Intelligence Estimate on Soviet Bloc; Soviet assistance to extremist groups; radical states supported by Soviet Bloc; Soviet support for political movements in Western Europe; East Germany and Bulgaria involvement in terrorism; Soviet Union and transnational terrorist activities; Soviet Union and Marxist groups; Soviet Bloc and foreign extremist groups;

# Publisher's Notes

Many observers born after 1970 are not aware of the Soviet Union's integral role in spreading terrorism throughout the world and consequently do not appreciate the through line between Soviet aggression and the modern Palestinian reliance on political violence. This 1986 National Intelligence Estimate provides an essential primer.

This annotated edition illustrates the capabilities of the AI Lab for Book-Lovers to add context and ease-of-use to manuscripts. It includes several types of abstracts, building from simplest to more complex: TLDR (one word), ELI5, TLDR (vanilla), Scientific Style, and Action Items; essays to increase viewpoint diversity, such as Grounds for Dissent, Red Team Critique, and MAGA Perspective; and Notable Passages and Nutshell Summaries for each page.

# Abstracts

## TL;DR (one word)

Support.

## Explain It To Me Like I'm Five Years Old

Sure! Let's break it down into simple words:

The Soviet Bloc was a group of countries that were friends with the Soviet Union, a big and powerful country. These countries sometimes helped bad groups and countries that wanted to make trouble or start fights in other places around the world. They did this because they wanted to spread their ideas and make more friends who believed in the same things they did.

Some countries in the Soviet Bloc, like Bulgaria and East Germany, were more involved in helping these bad groups than others. They gave them things like money, weapons, and training. This made it easier for those groups to do bad things in other countries, like causing explosions or hurting people.

The Soviet Union and its friends did these things because they wanted to support other people who believed in their ideas, even if it meant helping those who did dangerous things. They thought it was important to help these groups to make their ideas stronger and more popular around the world.

## Synopsis

This National Intelligence Estimate, issued in August 1986, delves into the intricate relationship between the Soviet Bloc and international terrorism and revolutionary violence. The document provides an in-depth analysis of Soviet attitudes and policies towards various forms of political violence, particularly those employed by groups they support. It sheds light on the factors influencing Soviet decisions regarding the backing of extremist groups, ranging from their potential effectiveness and alignment with Soviet interests to concerns about international reputation and potential backlash.

The estimate highlights the sophisticated and adaptable nature of Soviet support for such groups, emphasizing the utilization of allies and radical states to camouflage their involvement and maintain plausible deniability. It examines specific regional contexts, including the Middle East, Latin America, and other parts of the Third World, providing insights into the nuances of Soviet and allied support for various actors, such as the PLO in the Middle East and insurgent movements in Latin America. The document also analyzes the role of surrogates like Cuba and East Germany in furthering Soviet aims, highlighting their contributions to training, arming, and providing logistical support to these groups.

Furthermore, the estimate delves into the dynamics between the Soviet Union and radical states like Libya and Syria, exploring the limits of Soviet influence over their actions, particularly concerning terrorism. It also examines the complexities of the Soviet relationship with Cuba, acknowledging Cuba's relative autonomy in supporting revolutionary groups, sometimes even those at odds with Soviet-backed factions. The document concludes by analyzing trends in political violence, noting a decline in leftwing revolutionary activities while recognizing the rise of state-sponsored and ethno-religious terrorism, and assesses future prospects, suggesting a continuation of existing patterns and the enduring nature of Soviet support for extremist groups, contingent on a calculated assessment of costs and benefits.

## Scientific Style

**Abstract:**

The involvement of the Soviet Bloc in international terrorism and revolutionary violence has been an area of significant concern, as evidenced by the National Intelligence Estimate. The Soviet Union, alongside its Eastern European allies, notably Bulgaria and East Germany, has been actively supporting various extremist groups and radical states. This support includes political, financial, and logistical assistance, which has notably impacted groups operating in Western Europe. Despite occasional diplomatic rhetoric suggesting otherwise, the Soviet Bloc's commitment to fostering Marxist ideologies through transnational terrorist activities remains steadfast. The intricate network of aid and collaboration underscores the strategic importance placed by the Soviet Bloc on leveraging revolutionary violence as a tool for geopolitical influence and ideological dissemination.

## Action Items (Prospective)

- **Reflect on Historical Context:** Consider the geopolitical climate of the Cold War era, including the motivations and strategies of both the Soviet Bloc and Western nations. Understanding this context can provide deeper insights into the dynamics of international terrorism and revolutionary violence.

**Compare with Present-Day Situations:** Analyze how the historical support of extremist groups by the Soviet Bloc parallels or differs from modern-day state-sponsored terrorism. This can help in understanding current international relations and security concerns.

**Engage in Further Research:** Dive deeper into specific cases mentioned in the document, such as the roles of Bulgaria and East Germany. Research additional sources to get a more comprehensive view of these countries' involvement in supporting foreign extremist groups.

**Discuss with Peers or Experts:** Join discussion groups or forums focused on

Cold War history, international relations, or terrorism studies. Engaging with others can provide new perspectives and enhance your understanding of the material.

**Apply Learnings to Modern Policy Analysis:** Use the insights gained from the document to critically evaluate contemporary foreign policies and international security strategies. This can be particularly useful for students, professionals, or anyone interested in the fields of political science, international relations, or security studies.

# Viewpoints

*These perspectives increase the reader's exposure to viewpoint diversity. No endorsement of any particular view is intended.*

## Three Most Important Takewawys for Present-Day Readers

Here are three important takeaways from the 1986 NIE that can be applied to modern Russian foreign policy:

1. **The Soviet Union's strategic use of violence as a tool of foreign policy remains relevant.** The NIE demonstrates that the Soviets viewed violence not as a moral issue, but as a tactical one, to be used when advantageous. This perspective is reflected in modern Russian foreign policy, which often uses military force, proxy conflicts, and information warfare to achieve its goals. Examples include the annexation of Crimea, the support of separatists in eastern Ukraine, and the use of cyberattacks against Western institutions.

2. **Moscow's focus on maintaining a "plausible denial" of involvement in supporting extremist groups persists.** The NIE reveals that the Soviets often used surrogates and allies to provide support to foreign extremist groups, enabling them to deny direct involvement. This tactic remains a hallmark of Russian foreign policy. The use of private military companies, disinformation campaigns, and ambiguous support for various international actors obfuscates Russia's direct role in destabilizing activities.

3. **While Russia may publicly condemn terrorism, it often operates in a gray area of international norms.** The NIE underlines the contradiction between the Soviet Union's public condemnation of terrorism and its support for groups that engage in terrorist activities. Similarly, modern Russia often walks a fine line. It publicly condemns terrorism, yet maintains a relationship with certain actors who engage in it, and uses similar tactics to advance its own objectives. This creates a complex and challenging landscape for international relations, where Russia's actions and rhetoric are frequently at odds.

## Grounds for Dissent

As a member of the team that contributed to the National Intelligence Estimate on "The Soviet Bloc Role in International Terrorism and Revolutionary Violence," I must present a principled dissent to several of the claims made in the report. While the document posits that the Soviet Bloc, including countries like Bulgaria and East Germany, provides substantial support to foreign extremist groups and radical states, there are critical aspects and nuanced realities that the report has not fully considered.

Firstly, the assertion that the Soviet Union and its allies are deeply involved in supporting international terrorist activities is overly generalized and lacks sufficient empirical evidence. While it is true that the Soviet Bloc had ideological and occasionally material ties with certain revolutionary movements, the extent and nature of this support are often overstated. Many of the groups that engaged in "terrorist" activities were not directly controlled or significantly influenced by Soviet directives. Rather, these groups had their own local and nationalistic motivations that were often independent of Soviet interests. For instance, the PLO's activities in the Middle East and the Red Brigades in Italy had complex motivations that were not reducible to mere Soviet manipulation.

Moreover, the report does not adequately consider the geopolitical context of the Cold War, wherein both the United States and the Soviet Union engaged in proxy conflicts and supported various groups for strategic purposes. The focus on Soviet support for extremist groups omits a balanced discussion of how Western powers similarly backed certain factions that could be considered as engaging in revolutionary violence or terrorism. For example, the U.S. support for the Contras in Nicaragua and the Mujahideen in Afghanistan involved substantial assistance to groups that employed violent tactics against established governments.

Additionally, the document fails to address the internal dynamics within the Soviet Bloc countries themselves, which often constrained their ability to uniformly support international revolutionary violence. The political and economic turmoil within the Eastern Bloc in the late 1970s and 1980s meant that these countries were frequently preoccupied with their internal stability and governance challenges. This internal focus detracted from their capacity to effectively engage in or support international terrorism on a significant scale.

Furthermore, the report's implications that Soviet involvement in international terrorism is a monolithic and deliberate strategy do not fully align with the historical evidence. Instances of Soviet support were often inconsistent and opportunistic rather than part of a coherent long-term strategy. For example, Soviet backing of certain movements was sometimes more about countering Western influence rather than a genuine commitment to fostering revolutionary violence globally.

In conclusion, while the Soviet Bloc did have interactions with various radical and extremist groups, the narrative presented in the report is overly simplistic and fails to account for the multifaceted and often contradictory nature of these relationships. A more nuanced analysis should consider the local motivations of these groups, the comparable actions of Western powers, the internal constraints within the Soviet Bloc, and the opportunistic rather than strategic nature of Soviet support. Addressing these factors would lead to a more balanced and comprehensive understanding of the Soviet Bloc's role in international terrorism and revolutionary violence.

## Red Team Critique

Red Team Plan:

**Exploitation of Single Points of Failure:**

- **Communication Networks:** Target and disrupt the communication channels between the Soviet Bloc and their supported extremist groups. Cyber-attacks on communication infrastructure can create confusion, delay operations, and sever essential strategic coordination.

- **Supply Lines:** Identify and sabotage critical supply chains for arms and funds that the Soviet Bloc channels to these terrorist groups. Target key logistical hubs and transit routes to create bottlenecks and shortages.

- **Leadership Decapitation:** Focus on identifying and neutralizing key leaders within the extremist groups and their Soviet handlers to create leadership vacuums and disrupt operational continuity.

**Exploitation of Asymmetric Vulnerabilities:**

- **Cyber Warfare:** Launch cyber-attacks against Soviet Bloc nations to disrupt their critical national infrastructure, including financial systems, transportation networks, and energy grids. This will divert their attention and resources from international operations.

- **Ideological Subversion:** Utilize psychological operations (psyops) to undermine the ideological legitimacy of these groups. Spread misinformation and create internal conflicts within these terrorist organizations to weaken their cohesion and effectiveness.

- **Proxy Conflicts:** Support anti-Soviet insurgent groups within Soviet Bloc nations and allied states. This will stretch their resources thin as they deal with internal conflicts while trying to maintain external terrorist operations.

**Exploitation of Unsustainabilities:**

- **Economic Strain:** Implement economic sanctions and trade embargoes targeting key industries and financial interests of Soviet Bloc nations. This will create internal economic hardships and limit their ability to fund and support terrorist activities.

- **Allied Dependence:** Pressure and incentivize the Soviet Bloc's allies to reduce or cease their support for international terrorism, thereby isolating the Soviet Union diplomatically. Publicize and expose the negative impacts of these alliances to create public and political pressure on these governments.

- **Diplomatic Isolation:** Use international fora to consistently highlight and condemn Soviet support for terrorism. Mobilize a coalition of nations to impose comprehensive measures against states supporting terrorism, thereby increasing the political cost for the Soviet Union.

**Exploitation of Political Fragilities:**

- **Internal Dissidence:** Amplify and support dissident movements within Soviet Bloc nations. Highlight the regime's unpopular policies and human rights abuses to fuel internal unrest and dissent.

- **Exposing Corruption:** Publicize incidents of corruption and mismanagement within the Soviet Bloc governments to undermine their credibility and authority internally and internationally.

- **Alliance Disruption:** Work to create rifts between the Soviet Union and its closest allies by exploiting differences in national interests, historical grievances, and ideological inconsistencies. Use diplomatic channels to negotiate with more pragmatic elements within these alliances to foster defection or neutral positioning.

**Innovative Strategies:**

- **AI and Data Analytics:** Utilize advanced AI and data analytics to predict and preempt Soviet Bloc strategies and terrorist activities. This will allow for more targeted and timely countermeasures.

- **Public Awareness Campaigns:** Launch global awareness campaigns to inform the international public about the Soviet Bloc's role in supporting terrorism. Use social media, traditional media, and diplomatic channels to shape public opinion against the Soviet Union and garner global support for countermeasures.

- **Enhanced Intelligence Sharing:** Establish and enhance intelligence-sharing networks among global allies to improve the detection, interception, and neutralization of terrorist plots with Soviet connections.

By systematically targeting these vulnerabilities and applying pressure on multiple fronts, we can effectively counter the Soviet Bloc's strategy and diminish their capacity to support international terrorism and revolutionary violence.

# MAGA Perspective

*In an increasingly polarized market for English-language books, it must be assumed that readers will often come into contact with views of the topic that are that deeply skeptical of conventional wisdom. Consider this section an inoculation.*

The National Intelligence Estimate on the Soviet Bloc's role in international terrorism and revolutionary violence is nothing more than a relic of Cold War paranoia and leftist hypocrisy. MAGA supporters know that the real danger to America's freedom and security isn't some mystical Red Menace from decades past, but the radical leftists within our own borders who aim to dismantle everything this country stands for. This document, with its fixation on Soviet influence, ignores the modern-day threats posed by Antifa and other domestic terrorist groups that are actively supported and funded by powerful elites within our own government and media.

Despite the document's exhaustive focus on Soviet-backed terrorism, let's not kid ourselves: the real puppeteers of chaos and violence today are the progressive oligarchs who control Silicon Valley, Wall Street, and Hollywood. These people are far more dangerous than any external threat, as they wield unparalleled power to shape public opinion, suppress free speech, and promote their radical agenda. The so-called intelligence community would do well to turn its attention to these domestic enemies of the state, rather than continuing to chase ghosts from a bygone era.

The Soviet Bloc's alleged support for terrorism is laughable when compared to the rampant lawlessness allowed to flourish in American cities today under the guise of "social justice." Where is the National Intelligence Estimate on the role of leftist billionaires in bankrolling organizations that incite riots, loot businesses, and attack law enforcement? The selective blindness of the intelligence apparatus reveals a deep-seated bias and unwillingness to confront the real sources of revolutionary violence threatening America from within.

Furthermore, this document reeks of double standards. While it denounces Soviet assistance to foreign extremist groups, it turns a blind eye to the U.S. government's own history of meddling in other nations' affairs. From Vietnam to the Middle East, the American military-industrial complex has left a trail of destruction far worse than anything attributed to the Soviets. The hypocrisy is evident: it's acceptable for the U.S. to use force and subversion, but when another power does it, it's labeled terrorism.

In the end, this National Intelligence Estimate serves as a convenient distraction, diverting attention from the true threats facing America: a corrupt, power-hungry elite determined to undermine the values of freedom, sovereignty, and democracy. It's high time we recognize that the battle for America's future won't be won by fighting Cold War-era ghosts, but by standing up to the modern-day tyrants who seek to destroy our way of life from the inside out.

# The Soviet Bloc Role in International Terrorism and Revolutionary Violence

National Intelligence Estimate

NIE 11/2-86
August 1986

**THIS ESTIMATE IS ISSUED BY THE DIRECTOR OF CENTRAL INTELLIGENCE.**

**THE NATIONAL FOREIGN INTELLIGENCE BOARD CONCURS, EXCEPT AS NOTED IN THE TEXT.**

*The following intelligence organizations participated in the preparation of the Estimate:*

The Central Intelligence Agency, the Defense Intelligence Agency, the National Security Agency, and the intelligence organizations of the Department of State.

*Also Participating:*

The Assistant Chief of Staff for Intelligence, Department of the Army

The Director of Naval Intelligence, Department of the Navy

The Assistant Chief of Staff, Intelligence, Department of the Air Force

The Director of Intelligence, Headquarters, Marine Corps

Warning Notice
Intelligence Sources or Methods Involved
(WNINTEL)

NATIONAL SECURITY INFORMATION
Unauthorized Disclosure Subject to Criminal Sanctions

DISSEMINATION CONTROL ABBREVIATIONS

| | |
|---|---|
| NOFORN– | Not Releasable to Foreign Nationals |
| NOCONTRACT– | Not Releasable to Contractors or Contractor/Consultants |
| PROPIN– | Caution—Proprietary Information Involved |
| ORCON– | Dissemination and Extraction of Information Controlled by Originator |
| REL . . .– | This Information Has Been Authorized for Release to . . . |

| | |
|---|---|
| DERIVATIVE CL BY | |
| REVIEW ON | OADR |
| DERIVED FROM | Multiple |

SECRET

25X1

# NIE 11/2-86

# THE SOVIET BLOC ROLE IN INTERNATIONAL TERRORISM AND REVOLUTIONARY VIOLENCE

Information available as of 14 August 1986 was used in the preparation of this Estimate, which was approved by the National Foreign Intelligence Board on that date.

## CONTENTS

| | Page |
|---|---|
| SCOPE NOTE | 1 |
| KEY JUDGMENTS | 5 |
| DISCUSSION | 11 |
|     The Soviet Approach to Political Violence | 11 |
|     Soviet Attitudes and Policies Toward Terrorism | 13 |
|     Attitudes and Policies of Soviet Allies | 15 |
|     The Middle East | 19 |
|     Latin America | 22 |
|     The Rest of the Third World | 24 |
|     The Developed Countries | 25 |
|     Trends and Implications | 25 |
| Outlook | 26 |

## SCOPE NOTE

This Estimate supersedes SNIE 11/2/81, *Soviet Support to International Terrorism and Revolutionary Violence*. In this Estimate, *terrorism* means premeditated, politically motivated violence directed against noncombatant targets by nongovernment groups or clandestine state agents, generally to intimidate a target audience.[1] *International terrorism* involves citizens or territory of more than one country. *Transnational terrorism*, a kind of international terrorism, means attacks by terrorists outside their own homelands. *Revolutionary violence* is aimed at changing the fundamental political orientation of a society by force.

Since the SNIE presented an adequate historical treatment of the issue, in preparing this Estimate, we have concentrated on the developments of the past few years. At the same time, we have expanded the scope of the study to include related activities on the part of:

— *The rest of the Warsaw Pact countries*. In this Estimate the term "Soviet Bloc" means the Warsaw Pact countries.

— *Other Soviet allies* such as Cuba, Angola, Vietnam, and—to the extent their activities may have been undertaken in conjunction with the USSR—Libya and Syria.

We have also deemphasized the categorization of groups that engage in terrorism. The 1981 SNIE distinguished rather firmly between revolutionary insurgent groups and strictly terrorist groups, while acknowledging that many insurgent groups use terrorist tactics, and many terrorist groups have revolutionary goals. In this Estimate we focus on the nature of the support rather than on the nature of the groups per se. Our approach is to divide the world's non-Communist countries into clusters according to their predominant forms of political extremism:

— *The Middle East*. Most of the political violence originating in this region is an outgrowth of three independent—though overlapping—transnational phenomena: the Palestinian problem, radical Islamic fundamentalism, and the growing use of terrorism by states such as Syria, Libya, and Iran. Many of the

---

[1] This definition implicitly excludes violent acts by overt government organizations, officials, or agents.

extremist groups of the region routinely attack foreigners and operate outside their own countries, especially in Western Europe; thus they are often labeled international or transnational terrorist groups.

— *The Rest of the Third World.* Most of the political violence originating in other Third World countries is associated in some way with rebellion against national governments. The violent opposition groups operate almost exclusively in their own countries, although some have bases in sympathetic neighboring countries, and some attack foreign as well as domestic targets. Rebel groups in these countries are often able to establish control over regions or resources—usually in rural areas—beyond the reach of central government authority, thereby acquiring the status of insurgent groups.

— *The Developed Countries.* In general, the democratic Western countries have strong, stable political systems that, though governments may fall, are highly resistant to violent change. Nevertheless, leftwing extremist groups are active in a good number of West European countries and in Japan. In some Western countries, violent separatist and irredentist groups are also a problem. Many of the rebels in developed countries are ideologically indistinguishable from Third World insurgents and would be insurgents themselves if they could, but since it is not feasible for them to take and hold territory, they do not qualify as insurgents and are usually called terrorists.

**SECRET**

25X1

25X1

*This information is Secret* 25X1

## KEY JUDGMENTS

The Soviet leaders' approach to terrorism derives from their broader view that violence is a basic, legitimate tool of political struggle to be applied or sponsored in those settings where its use will benefit the USSR. As a result, the Soviets have no moral compunctions about supporting foreign insurgent and terrorist groups; the primary consideration is whether the activities of these groups further Soviet interests.

The Soviets support some groups openly and directly, mainly those with some claim to international political legitimacy, such as the PLO or the South-West African People's Organization (SWAPO). In dealing with many foreign political extremist groups, though, the Soviets camouflage much of their involvement by working with and through allies and radical states. To the extent that some of these states engage in terrorism or support extremist groups on their own accounts, the precise Soviet role is further obscured.

Though Moscow's dealings with foreign political extremist groups are highly differentiated, in general they follow these basic patterns:

— The Soviets support Palestinian and other radical anti-Israeli and anti-US groups based in the Middle East; most of them use terrorism as a means of seeking political objectives.

— The Soviets back insurrectionary movements in susceptible Third World states. Moscow refers to these organizations as national liberation movements; many of them engage in terrorist activities.

— The Soviets are not identifiably involved with terrorist groups in Western Europe and other developed areas where, more often than not, leftwing political violence interferes with Moscow's broad regional aims. Such violence does, however, create disruption that damages Western interests. Another view holds that the Soviets believe that, in most cases, terrorism in Western Europe furthers their aims. Moscow expects it to have a destabilizing effect on Western Europe and to undermine the US military posture there.[2]

---

[2] *The holders of this alternative view are the DIA, Army, Navy, Air Force, and Marine Corps.*

— Moscow's East European allies generally follow the Soviet lead in their own dealings with foreign insurgent and terrorist groups. In some cases they act as Soviet surrogates; in other cases they appear to be acting on their own. Other Marxist states in the Soviet orbit, particularly Cuba, also cooperate with the USSR in helping favored extremists groups around the world, but they tend to be more independent than the East Europeans.

*In the Middle East*, the Soviets and their associates provide much of the military support for various factions of the PLO. Though Palestinian "military" operations consist mainly of terrorist attacks, so long as such attacks are confined to Israel and the Occupied Territories the Soviets seem rarely to object. Available evidence, however, suggests:

— That the Soviets disapprove of terrorist attacks in Western Europe by Middle Eastern groups they support and have tried to discourage these groups from conducting such attacks.

— That the Soviets have avoided direct contact with Middle Eastern transnational terrorist groups outside the PLO, such as the Abu Nidal Group, the PFLP—Special Command, and the Carlos Apparat.

— That, conversely, several East European states—East Germany, Hungary, Romania, Bulgaria—have had direct ties to such groups. Their reasons appear to have been mainly defensive, but in some cases they may also have anticipated using the groups for their own or for Soviet purposes. Moscow certainly knew of some of these arrangements and presumably acquiesced. Another view holds that arrangements made by East European Communist regimes with transnational terrorist groups, in particular those arrangements between Hungary and Romania and the Carlos Apparat, serve a useful political purpose and further broad Communist objectives, but stresses that they are not mainly for defensive reasons.[3]

*In the Third World*, the USSR and its allies—notably Cuba, East Germany, and Bulgaria—provide training, weapons, funding, guidance, and other forms of support to numerous Marxist insurgent and terrorist groups. Chief among the target countries are Chile, Colombia, El Salvador, Guatemala, and Sudan. In general, the Soviets and East Europeans advocate revolutionary violence mainly when that appears to be the most promising option; the Cubans and Nicaraguans are more optimistic, viewing violence as a way to create new and promising options.

---

[3] *The holders of this alternative view are the DIA, Army, Navy, Air Force, and Marine Corps.*

Most of the radical Middle Eastern states—those that use terrorism as a foreign policy tool—are fundamentally dependent on the Soviet Bloc for military and political support. The list includes Syria, South Yemen, and Libya, along with elements in Lebanon; Iran is a notable exception. The Soviets have supplied these states with large amounts of military equipment, often without enforcing controls on their end use; subsequently, some of this equipment has been acquired and used by terrorist and insurgent groups:

— Even without generous political and military support from the Soviet Union, states such as Syria and Libya would probably aid various foreign political extremist groups, but being more vulnerable to retaliation they would have to be more circumspect.

— Although the USSR probably does not instigate the terrorist acts of these states and their surrogates and may not approve of all of them, neither does it risk straining relations with them by trying to make them desist. It undoubtedly recognizes that such acts are usually more damaging to Western interests than to Soviet ones.

*In Western Europe*, as well as in other areas where democratic institutions are strong, the Soviets regard leftwing terrorism as generally not helpful—indeed often harmful—to their regional objectives. Hence the Soviet Bloc keeps its distance from indigenous West European groups such as the Red Army Faction of West Germany and Action Directe of France. By criticizing and ostracizing such "criminal terrorist groups," moreover, Moscow attempts to indicate that, like the Western countries, the USSR opposes and is trying to fight terrorism.

To date, however, the Soviet Bloc has generally opposed and obstructed Western efforts to establish effective international counterterrorism programs, in part because such programs might impede the activities of extremist regimes and groups the Soviets back:

— Much of the turmoil around the world is rooted in regional and local disputes of a political, social, or religious nature and has nothing to do with Communism. Many non-Communist extremists, however, have emulated the revolutionary model—and sometimes the terrorist tactics—employed by so many of the groups that receive Soviet Bloc assistance.

— Thus the longstanding Soviet support for political extremism in the Communist cause—and also in the Palestinian cause—has contributed to the development of an international climate in which alienated or frustrated activists of all political stripes tend to turn to violence readily, rather than as a last resort, and to use terrorist tactics to magnify their impact.

*Declining Trend.* The terrorist implosion in Lebanon and the growth in terrorism of Middle Eastern origin in Western Europe during the past few years have overshadowed a gradual drop in the amount and seriousness of terrorist and insurgent activity in many other parts of the world. Although international terrorist incidents have been increasing in frequency in recent years, spurred by state-sponsored Palestinian and Shi'ite extremists, indigenous terrorist activity—especially that associated with the extreme left—has been in decline not only in Western Europe but also in Latin America and other parts of the Third World. In a large number of important countries—Turkey, Italy, Brazil, Argentina, to name just a few—the terrorists of the 1980s are few and feckless, compared with their predecessors of previous decades.

## Outlook

While there is no indication that any massive or global upswing in terrorist activity is in the offing, we believe that various stimuli will prevent the level of political violence around the world from declining much further. The pattern of recent years has been that, as political extremism on behalf of some cause is brought under control in one country or region, as it usually is sooner or later, political extremism on behalf of some other cause has broken out somewhere else. Thus, at the moment the Montoneros and Tupamaros are quiet, while Sikh, Tamil, and Shi'ite radicals present major terrorist problems. We expect this pattern to persist.

*Little Change Expected in Soviet Role.* We also expect the Soviet Bloc to continue to support various foreign extremist groups and radical states. The costs to the Soviet Bloc of providing such support appear to be slight, whether in terms of money, reputation, influence, or risk. Often the benefits have also been meager, but in some cases the payoff has been substantial, for example, a peace initiative stalled, a pro-Western government besieged. Where the potential costs appear to outweigh the potential benefits, as in Western Europe, the Soviets simply refrain from getting involved. Given this situation, the Soviets have no reason to modify these durable and flexible policies—unless international developments modify the calculus. In Western Europe, for example, where the Soviets have generally kept their distance from extremist groups of all sorts, serious political instability in a country might tempt them into an adventurous relationship with local leftist revolutionaries.

Conceivably, even in the absence of any external impetus, the new Soviet leadership might decide to modify Moscow's longstanding policies of supporting foreign political extremists (when it approves of their goals) and of opposing multilateral efforts to make terrorist activities crimes under international law. General Secretary Gorbachev has gone on public record twice in recent months to criticize terrorism, and he has cautioned both Syria and Libya to avoid terrorist acts that might provoke the United States. Moreover, the Soviets have hinted they might be willing to discuss ways in which East and West can cooperate to combat transnational terrorism. On the other hand, the opportunistic Soviet conduct during the recent confrontation between the United States and Libya is one of several indications that, so far, the Gorbachev regime is quite like its predecessors when it comes to actions, as opposed to words.

*This information is Secret*

## DISCUSSION

### The Soviet Approach to Political Violence

1. Soviet leaders believe that violence is a natural and often necessary means of political struggle. Generally, they regard violence as a legitimate form of political action when used on behalf of causes they favor or by groups they support, but are likely to condemn violence as "criminal terrorism" when it is used on behalf of causes they dislike or by groups they oppose. Thus the Soviets have few if any moral compunctions about supporting foreign political extremist groups—including those that engage in what we call terrorism; the overarching consideration is whether the activities of these groups further Soviet interests.

2. *Sophistication and Flexibility.* Providing support to foreign extremist groups is just one of numerous Soviet tactics designed to gain influence and bring about desired developments—such as the destabilizing of hostile regimes—in foreign countries. In some countries it is the chief tactic; in others it is integrated with alternative tactics, such as diplomacy, trade, aid, subversion, propaganda, and assisting legal Communist parties. In still other countries, the Soviets advise against using terrorist tactics and appear to avoid all contact with violent leftwing groups because their activities are viewed as detrimental to Soviet interests. A few leftwing groups—such as Sendero Luminoso of Peru—reject the Soviets. In sum, quite similar groups in different countries attract widely different levels of Soviet support:

— *In the Middle East*, numerous radical governments and groups rely chiefly on terrorism to keep the fluid situation there from congealing into a pattern they would dislike. As a way of maintaining and extending its own influence in the Middle East, the Soviet Union supports many of these radical entities—especially the various elements of the Palestine Liberation Organization (PLO)—even though in many cases it does not fully agree with their fundamental aspirations.

— *In many Third World countries*, political institutions are weak and governments are potentially vulnerable to violent overthrow. Where prospects for a Marxist insurrection look promising—and where allies such as Cuba are available to take the lead, actually or ostensibly—the USSR supports leftwing insurgent groups, which it calls "national liberation movements." Many of them employ terrorist tactics. Even where prospects for the left are not promising, the Soviets may support such groups if their activities undercut Western influence. Because Cuba is often an enthusiastic partner, these practices are especially prevalent in Latin America.

— *In Western Europe and other developed countries*, where political institutions are generally strong and few if any governments are vulnerable to violent overthrow, the activities of leftwing extremist groups are probably seen by Moscow as generally not helpful—indeed often harmful—to their broad regional objectives. To be sure, terrorist attacks by these groups degrade US military morale and may complicate US relations with NATO allies. On the other hand, they also alienate potential supporters of the legal left while confirming moderates and conservatives in their fear of—and need to band together against—the radical leftist threat. In these countries, the Soviet Union discourages the use of violent tactics by the organizations with which it is in contact and apparently shuns all contact with indigenous terrorist groups—including those of the left.

3. In some situations the Soviet Union backs several competing extremist groups at the same time. For example, Moscow supports both pro- and anti-Arafat Palestinian groups, although not necessarily with equal vigor. In other situations, the Soviet Union may decline to back any extremist groups directly, even though its allies do so. In Peru, for example, the Soviets have no apparent contact with the Revolutionary Movement Tupac Amaru, but Cuba has praised the group publicly, and Nicaragua has reportedly trained some of its members. Furthermore, Tupac Amaru has reportedly furnished guerrillas for the America Battalion, the multinational combat unit established by the Cuban-backed Colombian insurgent group M-19.

4. In deciding whether or not to support a particular group directly, Moscow considers a number of factors:

— Whether the group appears able to deliver what it promises. The Soviets do not necessarily insist that the group have prospects of success; it may suit the USSR for the group simply to be a destructive or destabilizing influence. But the Soviets generally do not waste their time or money on groups that talk without delivering.

— Whether the group appears likely to succeed without Soviet backing. If they think so, the Soviets may try to jump on the bandwagon, offering support in return for future considerations. Even when they doubt that a group will succeed, the Soviets may hedge their bet by offering a little aid.

— Whether providing support for a given group would injure larger Soviet equities—for example, a valued relationship with the government opposing the group (as in Peru) or a carefully nurtured public posture of reasonableness (as in Western Europe).

— Whether, alternatively, providing support for a given group would enhance larger Soviet equities—for example, by taking pressure off a beleaguered ally such as Nicaragua or by forestalling any resolution of the Palestinian problem that excluded a Soviet role.

— Whether Soviet assistance to a given group is likely to become publicly known and, if so, whether it can be made to seem legitimate before the world community. For instance, Moscow justifies its well-known support for the South-West Africa People's Organization (SWAPO) on the grounds that SWAPO is recognized by the United Nations as representing the people of Namibia.

5. *Plausible Denial.* In many ways, the Soviets' support of political violence is like their conduct of espionage: they cannot realistically conceal that they do it, but in specific instances they may want to be able to make a plausible denial. Thus the USSR usually tries to work with and through allies and surrogates so that its own role is camouflaged. The impression to be conveyed is that a diffuse international revolutionary brotherhood—largely but not entirely Marxist—is supporting insurgencies that have arisen spontaneously as a consequence of legitimate grievances. In some cases the USSR may be sensitive to the possibility that, as a superpower trying to subvert Third World states, it will be regarded as an imperialist.

6. By allowing or arranging for surrogates to deal with foreign insurgent and terrorist groups, Moscow is sometimes able to maintain correct (if not necessarily cordial) relations with the very governments these groups are trying to overthrow. In addition, the Soviets may also maintain more or less overt relations with any legal, ostensibly nonviolent Marxist parties in these countries. It is likely that Soviet intelligence services have recruited agents of influence in these countries as well. Thus, concealing its role as a supporter of violent opposition groups in a given country permits the USSR to exert pressure or influence there in several ways at once. It also offers the opportunity to orchestrate subversive cooperation among the varied opponents of the target government. At the same time, Moscow is able to deny any responsibility for the terrorist activities of the more violent groups that its allies are supporting.

7. *Measured Support.* Soviet assistance to political extremist groups is always measured, never unreserved or open-ended. Usually, Moscow requires that a group earn its aid by demonstrating both operational effectiveness and growing indigenous and international support. If a group serves Soviet interests by simply creating unrest or even by merely presenting a threat, Moscow may apply less rigorous standards.

8. In some Latin American countries—Honduras, Venezuela, Ecuador—the number of Marxist extremists receiving any sort of Soviet Bloc or Cuban support seems very low, relative to the number needed to pose a realistic revolutionary threat. Providing support at such low levels may seem almost perfunctory, even ritualistic, as if it were just something done for the sake of Communist tradition. Perhaps that is a factor in certain cases. But we believe that in most cases it simply reflects the recognition by Moscow and its allies that most countries are not ripe for revolution, and that it may take years for revolutionary conditions to develop. Meanwhile, the Soviet Bloc strategy is to keep alive even small, weak Marxist revolutionary groups—to arm, train, and support them, on a modest scale, until local conditions become more favorable. When (if) that occurs, these groups are in place, able to recruit more insurgents, absorb more support, build a clandestine support network of their own, and—because of their head start—perhaps even seize the leadership of a popular rebellion.

## The East-West Dichotomy Over Terrorism

Superficial similarities in rhetoric mask fundamental differences in the ways that the East and the West view terrorism. At bottom, the Western position is absolutist, while the Eastern position is situational.

In the West, though this is often not admitted, terrorism is basically a *moral* issue. The well-known difficulty of achieving widespread agreement over what is meant by the term terrorism stems mainly from efforts to define it in morally neutral terms, when the definers themselves think of it in moral terms. That is, they regard certain types of violent acts as intrinsically *wrong* no matter what the goal (at least outside a combat situation). For example, most Western citizens—and their governments as well—hold that it is always wrong to attack "innocent" civilians or officially protected persons such as diplomats.

Individually, many East Bloc citizens probably share the repulsion Western citizens feel toward terrorism, but their governments regard terrorism as basically a *tactical* issue. The fathers of Communism held that, under appropriate circumstances—that is, where it would promote the Communist cause—it was not only permissible but advisable to foment terror. Most of the time, they thought, terrorism was counterproductive. Modern Communist leaders apparently think roughly the same way. We judge that they rarely approve of terrorist acts anywhere that arouse public outrage, regardless of the groups committing the acts or the goals they are trying to reach. Public outrage over the acts of Marxist-Leninist groups or Palestinian groups is generally not helpful to their causes.

The Soviets are well aware of Western views of what is permissible in a political cause, and it must be an important consideration in determining the tactics they advise their client groups to use or avoid. Undoubtedly, the Soviet willingness to join formally with other countries in international agreements to outlaw skyjackings (but not other forms of terrorism) was based in large measure on the conviction that skyjackings would almost never help a Marxist revolutionary cause.

There probably are other limited areas of terrorist activity, such as attacks against diplomats, which for the same reason the Soviets might be willing in principle to agree to outlaw as international crimes. In general, however, the Western view that violence is rarely justified except in combat situations is incompatible with the Soviet view that violence is justified whenever it produces the desired results.

## Soviet Attitudes and Policies Toward Terrorism

9. Here is what General Secretary Gorbachev had to say about terrorism during his address before the 27th Session of the CPSU Congress in February 1986.

*Undeclared wars, the export of counterrevolution in all its forms, political assassinations, hostage taking, hijacking of aircraft, explosions in streets, airports, or railway stations—this is the loathsome face of terrorism, which those inspiring it try to disguise with various kinds of cynical fabrications. The USSR rejects terrorism in principle, and is prepared to cooperate actively with other states in order to root it out. The Soviet Union will resolutely protect its citizens from acts of violence, and will do all it can to protect their lives, honor, and dignity.*

10. This condemnation of terrorism, while propagandistic, is unprecedentedly explicit for a Soviet leader. Nevertheless, if the Soviets actually have moral reservations about the use of terrorist tactics as this statement suggests, it has not been discernable in their conduct to date. It is more likely that the statement reflects growing Soviet concern over accusations that Moscow is somehow to blame for much of the terrorism that afflicts the world. As such, it was a continuation of Gorbachev's earlier arguments that the causes of tension and unrest around the world cannot be attributed to the Soviet Union. Indeed, in mentioning "undeclared wars and the export of counterrevolution" Gorbachev was trying to make the counterargument that this terrorism is actually the result of US policies.

11. *A Tactical, Opportunistic Approach.* Despite Gorbachev's comments, the Soviet Bloc continues to back a wide range of political extremist groups that routinely use such terrorist tactics. The Soviets rarely acknowledge that groups they support have been guilty of terrorism. Either they deny that such groups have been responsible for any terrorist activities that may have occurred, or they assert that the violence was legitimate (or at least defensible) in context, and therefore not terrorism. On the other hand, they are quick to cry terrorism when their own interests have been directly attacked, and they frequently condemn as terrorist the violent activities of groups and governments of which they disapprove.

12. Taken as a whole, the evidence indicates that Soviet reservations about terrorism have less to do with its propriety than with its utility. Soviet disapproval of

terrorist tactics such as hijackings of civil airliners and attacks on diplomatic facilities appear to be based primarily on the judgment that such tactics are usually counterproductive. Moreover, the Soviets have occasionally been victimized by such terrorism themselves. The Soviet claim to oppose other types of terrorism, such as assassinations of political leaders or the explosion of bombs in streets or other public places, is less credible. For example, several groups receiving Soviet Bloc support routinely explode bombs in public places.

13. If we cannot take the word of its leader as a true measure of the Soviet Union's policies toward terrorism, we can draw relevant conclusions from a long period of consistent Soviet behavior. In general:

— The Soviets are reluctant to restrict the tactics a Marxist (or Palestinian) insurgent group might use in its own homeland against the government it is trying to overthrow or against allies of that government. The Soviets do not explicitly advocate terrorism, but they believe that all is fair in "wars of national liberation." For Soviet-backed groups, terrorism seems to be basically a local option. The Soviets probably advise them that their terrorism should not be so vicious, indiscriminate, or ill considered as to alienate the masses, energize the opposition, or compromise the legitimacy of the revolutionary government they hope to establish—in other words, that their actions should not be counterproductive. But they are not expected to adhere to a code of conduct that excludes terrorism.

— The Soviets often frown on leftwing terrorism in a nonrevolutionary situation, because in their experience it discredits the "progressive" forces, alienates many of their prospective supporters, and strengthens their adversaries in the government. On the other hand, the Soviets may support or encourage terrorism in certain nonrevolutionary situations: to disrupt a target society, for example, or to punish a government for adopting policies that offend the USSR.

— The Soviets also appear to disapprove, in general, of transnational terrorism—attacks by political extremists outside their own homelands—of the sort currently identified with Abu Nidal, even though this terrorism has been on behalf of causes—or governments—Moscow supports. Conceivably, the Soviets have privately approved of particular transnational terrorist events—or even had some part in them—but we have never obtained any evidence of it.

— Finally, the Soviet Bloc has strongly opposed most Western efforts to make international terrorist activities a crime under international law, because this might cramp the style of Marxist insurgents.

14. Following are some examples of the Soviet approach toward terrorists that demonstrate the wide range of Soviet policies in this area. According to considerable and pursuasive, although not always conclusive, evidence:

— Moscow furnishes funding, equipment, weapons, training, and guidance to numerous Marxist insurgent groups in Latin America and Africa that rely heavily on terrorist tactics—attacks on civilian targets and noncombatants, sometimes including women and children. Some of these

### The Soviet Policy Toward Political Assassination

The Soviet view of violence as a legitimate form of political action is also demonstrated in the USSR's long history of involvement in assassinations of political enemies outside its borders. The targets have generally been Soviet and, latterly, East European defectors and emigres rather than foreign figures. Moscow's willingness to employ assassination has varied sharply over the years: from 1926 to 1960 there were more than 40 documented cases of Soviet political assassinations or kidnapings in the West; while from the early 1960s to the late 1970s there were none—although some may have occurred without our knowledge.

groups, presumably with Soviet approval, help defray operating expenses through robberies, extortion, and kidnapings of foreign businessmen and diplomats.

— The USSR provides major military and political support to several radical regimes—most notably those of Syria and Libya—that routinely engage in, and back groups that engage in, transnational terrorist activities. When, owing to their terrorist activities, these governments have found themselves threatened or isolated, the Soviets have often provided additional military equipment and expressions of political support.

— The Soviet Union foments terrorist activities by the Afghan intelligence service in Pakistan's border regions in order to punish Islamabad for supporting the Afghan rebels and to induce it to cease that support.

— Moscow evidently disapproves of the nihilistic new-left terrorists of Western Europe typified by the Red Army Faction (RAF) of West Germany, Action Directe of France, and the Communist Combatant Cells of Belgium and has no apparent contact with them. The harm they do with their attacks on NATO installations and personnel does not make up for how much they discredit the left and alienate moderates, thus damaging wider Soviet equities in Western Europe.

— The Soviets also appear to avoid all direct contact with transnational terrorist groups such as the Carlos Apparat and the Abu Nidal Group—although deeply clandestine relationships with such groups cannot be ruled out. Here the reason appears to be one of image rather than ideology: the Soviets do not want to be identified as backing groups that quite so openly flout international standards of civilized behavior.

— When Palestinian groups under Moscow's influence have conducted transnational terrorist campaigns, the Soviets have urged them to stop. Soviet disapproval may have helped dissuade groups such as the Popular Front for the Liberation of Palestine (PFLP) from renewing international terrorist activities. On the other hand, several Palestinian groups supported by the Soviets—Fatah, for example—have recently conducted transnational attacks without forfeiting Soviet aid.

### Attitudes and Policies of Soviet Allies

15. *The East Europeans.* For the most part, the East European members of the Warsaw Pact have been following general Soviet guidelines with regard to supporting (or not supporting) insurgent and terrorist groups around the world. The Soviets give them a good deal of latitude, however, as to how much and what kind of support they will render to which groups. Bulgaria and East Germany are more involved than the other East European states:

- *Bulgaria* seems to function mainly as a Soviet surrogate in dispensing goods and services to violent political extremist groups. Through its trading firm, Kintex, it is particularly active in the profitable gray arms market, both buying and selling weapons. Some of them—usually via middlemen—end up in the hands of insurgents and terrorists in numerous countries.

- *East Germany*, however, is the most active of the East European states in promoting and supporting Marxist-Leninist revolutions abroad. This appears to be largely voluntary—a way for East Germany both to please the Soviet Union and enhance its role on the world stage.

- Furthermore, East Germany can better afford such largess than *Czechoslovakia, Poland, and Hungary*, whose contributions to the cause of foreign revolutionary violence are consequently smaller.

- Unlike the other East European states, *Romania* operates independently of the USSR in its limited dealings with foreign revolutionary and extremist groups.

16. *The International Gray Arms Market.* This is the name given to a cluster of cutout mechanisms used to separate arms suppliers from their ultimate consumers, so they cannot be blamed if the arms are subsequently misused. Trading firms of the East European governments, especially Kintex of Bulgaria, are heavily involved in the gray arms market, which is a source of many of the small arms and light infantry weapons used by insurgents and terrorists. Generally, private arms dealers and brokers serve as middlemen for these trading firms, on whose behalf they buy Western-made weapons that via other middlemen the trading firms can resell—at a profit and for hard currency—to radical states and groups. The trading firms also use such middlemen to market Eastern-made weapons to radical states and groups with which the East Bloc governments do not wish to be directly identified.

## East European Dealings With Transnational Terrorist Groups

According to a number of reports from independent sources, some of indisputable authenticity, in the early 1980s certain East European governments established limited cooperative relationships with transnational terrorist groups based in the Middle East. Only one of these governments—Romania—is reported to have instigated any terrorist activity; generally they seem to have entered into these arrangements in order to keep track of, prevent local attacks by, and maintain some control over terrorists who were operating in their countries anyway. Thus they appear to be similar to reported look-the-other-way arrangements in effect during the same period between various terrorist groups and many West European governments including France, Italy, and West Germany.

— During the mid-1970s, the *Romanian* Government reportedly displayed consternation over suggestions that the infamous international terrorist Carlos (then an associate of the PFLP Special Operations Group) was operating freely from Romanian soil. ▓▓▓▓▓ however, the Romanian security service, ▓▓▓▓▓ had a formal relationship with the Carlos Apparat.

— In 1981, after Budapest discovered that the Carlos Apparat had been transferring weapons and equipment through *Hungary* without its knowledge, the Hungarian regime, ▓▓▓▓▓ made a formal arrangement with the terrorists. The group was given freedom of movement, allowed to operate workshops and other facilities, and permitted to transship weapons to the West on flights coming from the Middle East via Moscow. Carlos himself ▓▓▓▓▓ spent considerable time in Hungary and was said to have been in the country as recently as October 1984. In return, the Carlos Apparat was to report on Arabs in Hungary and desist from activities there while foreign dignitaries were visiting.

— A similar arrangement was ▓▓▓▓▓ worked out with the *East German* Government, but although agents of the Carlos Apparat occasionally operated out of East Berlin, the East Germans never allowed them the freedom of action they expected. As recently as August 1983, though, the group was implicated in an attack on the French cultural center in West Berlin—an attack presumably staged from its base in East Berlin.

— According to several apparently independent reports, the East Germans have also allowed the Abu Nidal Group to stage attacks out of East Berlin against representatives of Fatah, the Palestinian group headed by Yasir Arafat, with whom Abu Nidal has been feuding for a decade. (It is not clear why East Germany, which like the USSR supports Fatah, would facilitate attacks by the Abu Nidal Group against Fatah representatives.)

— The Carlos Apparat is said to have shipped weapons through *Bulgaria* with government knowledge

17. **Contacts With Terrorists**. Like the USSR, the East European countries appear in general to avoid direct involvement with the indigenous new-left terrorists of Western Europe. On one occasion, the Bulgarian Government even extradited four wanted members of the Red Army Faction to West Germany. On the other hand, there is persuasive—though not conclusive—evidence that, after Italy's Red Brigades kidnaped US Army Brigadier General Dozier in 1981, the Bulgarian intelligence service, working through an Italian agent of influence, offered to trade weapons and funds for information the group obtained from Dozier. For reasons not clear, this arrangement was never consummated. If the offer was genuine, however, it demonstrates that the Bulgarian Government, at least an element of that government, was willing to deal with such terrorists when it stood to benefit. (At the same time, of course, it also demonstrates the lack of existing East Bloc ties to the Red Brigades).

18. ▓▓▓▓▓ several East European governments had reportedly established limited cooperative arrangements with the Carlos Apparat and the Abu Nidal Group, two transnational terrorist groups based in the Middle East. Except for Bucharest, which, ▓▓▓▓▓ targeted agents of the Carlos Apparat against certain dissident Romanian emigres in Western Europe, there is no indication that these governments exercised any direction over these groups. We suspect that, instead, the East Europeans sought to monitor and constrain the activities of these groups in their own countries and to ensure that they would not be implicated in any terrorist acts these groups committed elsewhere.

## East European Dealings With Transnational Terrorist Groups (Continued)

but does not have any specific arrangements with the Bulgarian service. In general, Bulgaria's involvement with transnational terrorist groups seems limited to weapons sales through third parties. during the early 1980s the Bulgarian Government asked the PFLP to provide training to a Turkish terrorist group.

According to the fragmentary evidence in our possession, the Soviets played no part in making these alleged arrangements. Some reports indicate, moreover, that Moscow has maintained a hands-off attitude toward them. when the Hungarians approached the Soviets for advice on how to reconcile their arrangement with the Carlos Apparat with their new membership in Interpol, the Soviets declined even to offer advice. Yet, it is possible that in some of these cases East European officials may have been acting at Soviet behest. We would be unlikely to obtain evidence of this; even leaders of the government in question would not necessarily be fully aware of the Soviet role. If the Soviets did want to support or use groups of such ill repute, they would be likely to try to work through controlled East European cutouts. Since the working relationships between Soviet intelligence and security services and their counterparts in Eastern Europe vary from country to country, this is more feasible in some countries than others:

— The relationship between the Soviet and Romanian services is poor, and Ceausescu is known to keep close tabs on it—as well as on what his security services are up to. The Romanians are very unlikely to have been acting on behalf of the Soviets or without the knowledge of Ceausescu.

— The relationships between the Soviet services and other East European services are warmer, in some cases, much warmer. Yet there are some significant differences among countries. While the East German services cooperate closely with the Soviets, they also operate independently, and they are believed to do very little of consequence without the knowledge and approval of Honecker. Whether the reported East German dealings with international terrorists were self-initiated or at the behest of the Soviets, the East German leadership probably would have been fully informed.

— The Bulgarian and Hungarian services also work closely with the Soviets, but they appear to operate on a longer leash from their own governments than the Romanian or East German services. Their top leaders would not necessarily be aware of particular joint operations between their services and those of the Soviets. Alternatively, they could be aware and just look the other way.

On the face of it, there does not appear to be much reason for Moscow to take the risk of becoming involved even indirectly with such essentially self-motivated, erratic, and uncontrollable elements as the Carlos Apparat. If the Soviets wished for some reason to conduct terrorist acts, they have much more covert, reliable, and effective assets available. Although Carlos attended Lumumba University in his youth and at one time was reportedly at least considered for recruitment by the KGB, the Soviets have publicly expressed disapproval of the terrorist activities with which Carlos later became so prominently identified. Carlos was placed on the official watchlist of aliens forbidden to enter the Soviet Union.

19. The available evidence suggests that the Soviets had nothing to do with setting up these arrangements, although the East European governments probably believed they were acceptable to Moscow. Certainly, the KGB (thus some Soviet leaders) must have been aware of them. On at least one occasion, the Soviets reportedly tried to pass information, via an East European government and its contacts in the Carlos Apparat, to the Armenian terrorist group ASALA, warning it not to conduct any activities in East Bloc territory. It is possible—though not documented—that in some of these cases, the East European governments were acting as Soviet surrogates.

20. Compared with the Soviet Union, *Cuba and Nicaragua* appear to have less respect for the objective conditions that (the Soviets believe) must obtain before a Marxist revolution can succeed. Basically, Cuba and Nicaragua seem to think that a revolution can be jump started—that the right mix of leadership, organization, training, discipline, political agitation, and violence can succeed even in less-than-ideal circumstances. Until the Sandinistas came to power in Nicaragua in 1979, the Cubans were well in front of the Soviets in promoting Marxist insurgencies in Latin America. Since then, Moscow has moved closer to Havana's position. Nevertheless, Cuba continues to support a number of Latin American groups that, judging by the lack of Soviet interest in them, Moscow believes to have no realistic prospects. The level of Nicaraguan support to Marxist revolutionaries in Latin America is much lower than Cuba's, but that is apparently the result of a lack of resources, an inability to conceal

## The Soviet Bloc and the Radical States

*Libya.* In general, the Soviets have neither sought nor exercised much influence over the activities of Libya with regard to insurgent and terrorist groups. For all his reliance on Soviet arms, the mercurial, ambitious, and financially independent Colonel Qadhafi considers himself in competition with both Communism and Christianity. Thus he forms and nurtures African insurgent groups for his own reasons—chiefly a desire to dominate northern Africa and garner influence in the Third World. Similarly, he encourages and supports terrorist acts by Palestinian and other groups—especially the Abu Nidal Group—as a means of striking out at his enemies, notably Israel and the United States. Except, perhaps, for providing weapons, the Soviets have had nothing to do with the main sort of Libyan terrorism in Western Europe, the murder of Libyan dissidents by government agents. Officials of Libyan People's Bureaus have coordinated these attacks, in some cases carried them out.

Libya has been cooperating in a limited fashion with the Soviet Union, Cuba, and other Communist countries in helping Marxist insurgent groups in parts of Africa and Latin America, chiefly by providing money, weapons, and scholarships. In many places, however, especially in the Caribbean, Libyan agents appear to be working at cross purposes with the Soviets and Cubans. In general, they have been much less discriminating than the Communists and much more eager to promote violence in unpromising circumstances. Before crude oil prices crashed, when Tripoli had money, it seemed to be available to just about any anti-Western or antidemocratic extremist group that would send representatives to Libya, at Libyan expense, to receive training in paramilitary tactics and the tenets of Qadhafi (but neither Marx nor Lenin). During the recent confrontation between Libya and the United States, the Soviets offered Libya both materiel and rhetorical support but not what it needed—a commitment to defend Libyan territory from US reprisals. Tripoli has not earned such an open-ended commitment.

*Syria.* Although it receives considerable Soviet aid, especially military aid, Syria provides little practical help to the cause of Communist revolutions around the world. Damascus is involved in a wide variety of terrorism on its own behalf, however: its agents have murdered dissident Syrian emigres (mostly from the Muslim Brotherhood) in several West European countries; it has been the chief supporter of the Abu Nidal Group and the Carlos Apparat, as well as of some of the most militant of the Palestinian groups; it has instigated terrorist attacks against Middle East governments whose policies it opposes; it has allowed Shi'ite extremists from Iran and Lebanon to run terrorist recruiting and training sites in the part of Lebanon its forces control. Most recently, it has been implicated in terrorist bombings in West Berlin and in an effort to blow up an El Al airliner departing from London's Heathrow Airport. It is the substantial support provided to Syria by the USSR that enables the Assad regime to pursue these policies, which under other circumstances would be extremely reckless.

assistance at higher levels, and a perception of vulnerability to US reprisals rather than of any ideological differences between Managua and Havana.

21. *Vietnam* has provided small quantities of weapons from its huge stockpile of captured US arms. Moscow brokered at least one of these transactions. Hanoi reportedly has also provided instructors for insurgent training in Cuba and may have furnished training to a few Latin American insurgent cadre in Vietnam. *North Korea's* main contribution to foreign political violence over the years has been the stream of saboteurs and assassins it has tried to infiltrate into South Korea. In 1983, moreover, North Korean agents killed several South Korean Government officials by bombing a high-level South Korean delegation during its state visit to Rangoon. As regards support for foreign extremists, North Korea has provided guerrilla training in its own country to members of a number of Third World insurgent groups. From time to time, moreover, North Korean instructors have also been reported as conducting paramilitary training of leftist guerrillas abroad, sometimes in places like Angola and South Yemen, where Soviet influence is strong. In general, though, there is little evidence that North Korean dealings with Third World revolutionaries are coordinated with the USSR. In view of the warming of Soviet–North Korean relations in recent years, closer cooperation among them cannot be ruled out in the future.

22. Some Soviet Marxist allies are only involved with foreign extremists in their immediate neighborhoods. With Soviet Bloc help, *Ethiopia* provides shelter and assistance to insurgents in neighboring countries (Sudan, Somalia) whose governments furnish sanctuary and assistance to Ethiopian separatist groups. In collaboration with the USSR and Cuba, *Angola* offers haven and help for SWAPO and the ANC.

23. *Coordination*. New leftwing revolutionary groups—or political activists thinking of embarking upon an insurgency—might be able to shop around for support, perhaps obtaining help from Cuba after being turned down by the Soviets or East Germans. Indeed, it would appear to be the rare anti-US group that could not obtain at least some support from Cuba or Libya. Once a number of Soviet Bloc countries become deeply involved, however—perhaps one country providing training; a second providing weapons; a third providing doctors, nurses, and teachers; a fourth providing money; a fifth providing safehouses and sanctuary—there is a need to coordinate the aid, as well as what is demanded of the recipients in return. We have little information about the coordinating process, but it is probably much more complicated than the Soviet representative simply issuing orders. Nevertheless, since the Soviets are the ultimate source of much of the wherewithal, they obviously have considerable influence over what happens to it. But also apparently important are the equities, capabilities, limitations, and inclinations of the other states involved.

### The Middle East

24. Some years ago, working with and through its Marxist government, the Soviet Union used South Yemen as a base from which to promote leftwing rebellions in a number of Middle Eastern countries, particularly North Yemen. These insurrections went nowhere. Since around 1982, the Soviets have been trying to regularize relations with the governments they had been trying to subvert. Support for Communist parties and liberation groups throughout the region has been somewhat deemphasized in favor of this more diplomatic approach, which can be expected to continue only so long as it pays dividends.

25. Unsubstantiated reports have occasionally surfaced alleging Soviet involvement with the Armenian Secret Army for the Liberation of Armenia (ASALA), a transnational terrorist group that originated in Beirut. According to reporting from more reliable sources, the Soviets have had little or nothing to do with ASALA, which is among the extremist organizations they refer to as "criminal terrorist groups." Similarly, occasional reports allege Soviet involvement with other Middle Eastern extremist groups. a suspected Soviet KGB officer had been observed in conversation with a senior member of the Lebanese Armed Revolutionary Faction (LARF). Much has subsequently been learned about the once shadowy LARF, however, without illuminating any Soviet hand in its activities. In fact, the only Middle Eastern extremist groups known to have received significant Soviet support in recent years are the paramilitary components of the PLO.

26. *The Wellspring of Terrorism*. The Palestinian extremists have contributed more than any other group to the proliferation of the terrorist ethic during the past two decades. They have offered a terrorist option to several weak but vicious Middle East regimes and have exposed a number of Middle East and West European governments as irresolute. Their example has both inspired and educated extremists from other ethnic groups—notably Armenians and Shi'ites—who have consciously emulated their tactics. They have provided both weapons and training to terrorists from dozens of countries and from across the entire political spectrum. They have served as role models to disaffected youths all over the world, suggesting not only that terrorism is a reasonable reaction to political frustration but also that terrorists are glamorous and heroic figures to whom normal laws and ethical considerations do not apply.

27. *The Soviets and the Palestinians*. The USSR has long been a staunch supporter of the Palestinian cause. Under Moscow's guidance, the other members of the Soviet Bloc have also aided the Palestinians. Although Arab states provide most of the financial underpinnings to the various Palestinian guerrilla groups, the Soviet Bloc provides much of the military assistance and training (along with other forms of aid such as academic scholarships). The training is in both conventional and unconventional military techniques. The latter are useful not only in military combat but also in terrorist operations—the chief distinction being not the technique but the target and context. Judging by target and context, what the Palestinians call "the armed struggle" in Israel and the occupied territories consists mostly of terrorism. Moscow appears to accept Palestinian terrorism inside the Israeli-occupied territories as justified but to disapprove of it elsewhere—to the point that during the 1970s the Soviets reportedly cut off aid to the PFLP because of its involvement in transnational terrorism. Another view holds that the Soviets probably never went so far as to cut off aid to the Popular Front for the Liberation of Palestine (PFLP) to express disapproval of PFLP involvement in transnational terrorism.[4]

28. It must be noted that the Palestinians do not actually need to get paramilitary training from the Soviets. They can also get it from various Arab regimes, and they are capable of conducting such training themselves. Perhaps as valuable as the mili-

---

[4] *The holders of this alternative view are the DIA, Army, Navy, Air Force, and the Marine Corps*

## Soviet Bloc Training of Insurgents and Terrorists

Personnel from numerous foreign insurgent and extremist groups have undergone military and paramilitary training in the Soviet Union and Eastern Europe, as well as in other Communist countries. The curricula have ranged from ideological indoctrination and various academic courses, through basic military science and infantry training, to advanced instruction in specialized conventional and unconventional warfare techniques and intelligence methods—and how to teach the same material to others.

Typically, the students are the cream of larger groups that have already received preliminary training in their own regions. Various factions of the PLO, for example, conduct training in several Middle Eastern countries. The ANC has training bases in Angola and Tanzania. Would-be insurgents from numerous Latin American countries often receive their first formal military instruction at camps in Cuba or Nicaragua. Many of the teachers at these local facilities are graduates of courses in the Soviet Bloc.

*Training Facilities.* Most of the sites in the Soviet Bloc that we have identified as providing training to personnel from foreign extremist groups are located at known military installations where indigenous military personnel, along with personnel from the armed forces of Soviet allies, are trained. Following are some well-documented examples in the USSR:

— *The Simferopol Army Barracks*, located near Sevastopol in the central Crimea, is the site of a school for Foreign Military Personnel. It has provided instruction in small unit tactics, artillery, engineer and chemical operations, antitank weapons, and communications to students from several African countries, as well as the PLO. During the 1970s, as many as 3,000 foreign students were trained there at once. Personnel from foreign insurgent and extremist groups composed only a small portion of the student body.

— *The Odessa Combined Arms Military Training School*, located on the northern coast of the Black Sea, houses the United Red Banner Higher Military Institute. It provides classroom instruction on artillery, armor, communications, engineering, chemical warfare, and basic military science to students from various Third World countries associated with the USSR, including Cuba, Angola, and Mozambique.

— *The Odessa Army Barracks*, located about 30 kilometers north of the Odessa Combined Arms Military Training School, serves as the field training area for students at that installation. It is the site of the Odessa Foreign Personnel Training Center, the field counterpart of the Red Banner Institute. In addition to conventional infantry training, the center reportedly offers various sorts of guerrilla warfare training.

— *The Solnechnogorsk Combined Arms Training Complex*, located about 60 kilometers northwest of Moscow, is a major Soviet ground force training center. Several sources have reported that students from various Latin American, Middle Eastern, and African insurgent and extremist groups have received training at this installation under GRU auspices.

— *The Moscow Army Barracks*, located about 30 kilometers east of Moscow, has been identified as a training site for paramilitary elements of the KGB. Established in the late 1970s, it was used originally to train counterterrorist units in preparation for

tary training is the sense imparted to the homeless Palestinians that they are accepted as equals among the world's "progressive" peoples. Indeed, the Soviet Bloc has accorded the PLO some of the recognition and privileges normally associated only with sovereign governments and helped to persuade the UN General Assembly to grant it special status as well.

29. The fragmentation of the PLO that occurred in the wake of the Israeli invasion of Lebanon presented the Soviets with a problem, since its policies had been based on a unified Palestinian front. Moscow's response was to try to paper over the split and to urge the antagonists (whose agents have been murdering each other all over Europe and the Middle East) to submerge their differences for the sake of the Palestinian cause. To try to ensure that, if some faction decisively wins the intramural struggle, it will be on good terms with that faction, Moscow has continued to provide aid to all elements in the dispute, thereby forfeiting much of the leverage its support might otherwise bring.

30. *Arafat Still Supported.* Because the portion of Fatah loyal to Yasir Arafat remains the largest of the guerrilla groups and because Arafat retains the allegiance of more Palestinians in the occupied territories than any other Palestinian leader, the Soviets have continued to recognize Arafat as the head of the PLO and to provide his organization with arms, training, and financial support—albeit at reduced levels since the Israeli invasion of Lebanon. On the other hand, it

## Soviet Bloc Training of Insurgents and Terrorists (Continued)

the 1980 Olympics in Moscow. Subsequently, Cubans, Angolans, Ethiopians, and Palestinians have reportedly received training at this installation, which appears to be oriented toward urban warfare operations.

— *The Special Center* in Moscow, which is run by the GRU, trains foreign students—who must be approved by the International Department of the CPSU Central Committee—in politics, subversion, intelligence methods, topography and map reading, diversionary tactics, and "methods of antipartisan struggle." We do not know whether these courses are taught right at the center or whether it organizes and manages courses taught at other locations.

— *Patrice Lumumba Friendship University* in Moscow is sometimes cited as a place where foreign terrorists go for training. Some citizens of Third World countries who attended Lumumba University may have subsequently turned out to be terrorists, although training offered there appears to consist primarily of academic subjects and ideological indoctrination.

### The Question of Terrorist Training

The essence of terrorism lies not in its violence, which is not markedly different from the violence encountered in military combat (or in nonpolitical crime), but in the target, the context, the motivation, and the goal. Although both soldiers and terrorists use weapons and explosives, terrorists do so outside a combat situation and against noncombatant targets. Nevertheless, many of the activities of terrorist groups are hardly distinguishable from normal military activities. Like military units, terrorist groups must be concerned not only with operations but also with personnel matters, logistics, intelligence, security, and public affairs. Most terrorist groups, in fact, characterize themselves as military organizations.

Thus, much conventional military training is directly applicable to terrorist activities. It is well documented that personnel from numerous foreign terrorist groups (that is, extremist groups that employ terrorist tactics) have received such training in Soviet Bloc countries. On the other hand, certain terrorist activities have no direct military counterparts—the skyjacking of civil airliners, for example, or the conduct of a hostage/barricade incident, or the assassination of a civilian target. We have no recent evidence that training in this sort of activity is offered in Soviet Bloc countries.

Between such terrorism-specific activities and conventional military activities, however, lies a vast array of unconventional warfare techniques. The improvisation of explosive and incendiary devices from household ingredients, the preparation of command-detonating and time-detonating systems, the sabotage of transport, power, and communications facilities, the raid, the ambush, the abduction, the hit-and-run attack—these are the staple techniques of rural insurgents and urban terrorists alike. Even in the West, unconventional warfare schools commonly teach such techniques, and we believe that those in the Soviet Bloc are no exception. Whether this constitutes "terrorist training" is a matter of context and interpretation.

---

is clear that Moscow prefers other groups to Fatah—especially the Democratic Front for the Liberation of Palestine (DFLP), the most avowedly pro-Soviet and doctrinaire Marxist of the Palestinian groups and among the least active in the terrorist arena. DFLP students reportedly are offered military and other forms of training not made available to students from other Palestinian groups.

31. The Soviet Bloc has also resumed aid to the PFLP, which spawned most of the international Palestinian terrorist groups and which has from time to time offered training and weapons to terrorists from Western Europe and other parts of the world. The concern that the Soviets would cut off aid again may have been a factor in dissuading the PFLP from resuming its international terrorist activities. But the Soviet Bloc does not appear averse to the PFLP (or other Palestinians) passing on its terrorist expertise to others. The Soviet Union may view the PFLP as a useful surrogate in the event it wants some terrorists to obtain training but does not want to be directly involved.

32. The Soviets and East Europeans also offer minor support, chiefly training, to other, lesser Palestinian guerrilla groups such as the PFLP-General Command (PFLP-GC), Sa'iqa, and the Syrian wing of the Palestine Liberation Front (PLF), but the support of local Arab patrons, especially Syria and Libya, is very important to these groups. Of course, many of the weapons they get from Syria and Libya originate in the Soviet Bloc.

## Latin America and the Caribbean

33. The Soviet Union, along with many of its allies, provides limited funding, training, weapons, and equipment directly to certain Latin American revolutionary groups. Moscow's chief contribution, however, is the military, economic, and political support it has long rendered Cuba and now provides Nicaragua. Havana and (to a much lesser extent) Managua train the bulk of leftwing Latin American insurgents and terrorists, provide safehaven for their leaders, strategists, and dependents, help them acquire and smuggle weapons, provide them with funds, medical support, intelligence, and false documentation, offer advice and encouragement, and facilitate contacts and arrangements among their organizations. Without the Soviet Bloc assistance and backing, neither country would be as able to perform its vanguard role in promoting revolution in Latin America.

34. Nevertheless, while both Cuba and Nicaragua are heavily dependent on the Soviets, their regional policies are also driven by the revolutionary zeal of their leaders, by hostility toward the United States, and—on Cuba's part—by a desire to be seen as a leading Third World state. Indeed, Havana has occasionally wanted to go further than Moscow in supporting the pursuit of armed struggle. The relationship between Moscow and Havana is complex:

- In addition to economic ties and shared ideology, the Soviet Union and Cuba are bound together by mutual geopolitical objectives, prominent among which is a desire to promote revolutionary change in Latin America. In pursuit of this goal, Soviet and Cuban officials exchange information, debate strategies, and coordinate general lines of policy. Sometimes they also work closely together; in many cases they work independently. For the most part, the Soviet Union supplies the funds for operations run by the Cubans.

- Although Cuba plays a vital role in Soviet strategy toward Latin America (and Sub-Saharan Africa as well), it is allowed latitude to pursue initiatives of its own, so long as this is accomplished in a fashion that complements Moscow's agenda. Thus Cuba enjoys the freedom to back revolutionary groups of its own choosing, sometimes even when these groups are rivals of groups backed by the Soviet Union. Undoubtedly, this latitude does not extend to Cuban operations that would create important difficulties for the Soviet Union. Moscow's equities in Peru, for example, not only prevent it from supporting Marxist extremists there but probably lead it to restrain Havana as well.

35. The success of the Sandinista revolution in 1979 led to the belief, not only among the Nicaraguans and Cubans but also among the Soviets and East Europeans, that conditions were ripe for leftist revolutions in several Central American countries. They greatly boosted their aid to Central American insurgent groups, especially in El Salvador. In addition, Moscow urged the pro-Soviet Communist parties of the region, which were generally engaged in nonviolent forms of political action, to establish combat units and join in the revolutionary struggle. Since then, however, leftwing extremist groups throughout the region have suffered a considerable number of military and political reverses. The increasing US involvement in Central America, along with the US operation in Grenada, demonstrated that under certain circumstances the United States would forcefully oppose Communist thrusts. Accordingly, both the Soviets and Cubans appear to have recognized that the conditions in most Central American and Caribbean countries are not as conducive to revolution as they had thought.

36. At present, four strains of Cuban and Soviet Bloc involvement with Latin American extremist groups may be distinguished:

- Ensuring the survival of the Sandinista regime in Nicaragua.

- Supporting the Marxist insurgents in El Salvador.

- Overthrowing the Pinochet regime and reestablishing a leftist government in Chile.

- Balancing limited support for a wide range of Marxist elements in other Latin American countries with improvement in state-to-state relations, especially with the recently established democracies.

37. The Soviets and Cubans seem to be trying to intensify the insurgent threat throughout Central America. In part, this is probably intended to prevent Washington from focusing its attention solely on Nicaragua. Concurrently, local states are induced to think twice before supporting counterrevolution in Nicaragua. Thus extremist groups in Guatemala, Honduras, and Costa Rica have been encouraged to unite with other like-minded groups and to undertake terrorist attacks against government and establishment targets in the hope of destabilizing their governments. On the

other hand, the insurgent groups of El Salvador have been advised to avoid an all-out confrontation with the Salvadoran military, because they might stimulate greater US support for the government. They have also been criticized by Havana for terrorist attacks such as the kidnaping of President Duarte's daughter, because it brings them bad publicity and alienates liberal sympathizers in Western countries.

38. In South America, the Castro regime has been on a diplomatic offensive of late, downplaying support for leftwing extremist groups in many countries in favor of establishing friendlier relationships with the governments they oppose. Judging that the circumstances in most of these countries are not favorable for revolution—either because the governments are strong or because the left is weak and divided—Havana has continued to offer training and limited funding to would-be guerrillas from some of these countries but seems to have advised most of them—except in Chile and Colombia—to bide their time. This has left a bit of an opening that Qadhafi has tried to exploit, by offering aid to extremist groups independent of that furnished by the Soviet Bloc and Cuba. So far, there is evidence that Cuba resents this Libyan meddling but not enough to modify significantly its current policy of modest restraint.

39. On the other hand, the Pinochet regime in Chile has been the object of Cuban subversion since Pinochet took power by overthrowing Salvador Allende in 1973. Of late, the Cubans have even been enlisting insurgent groups from other Latin American countries in the anti-Pinochet crusade. For example, Argentinian Montonero exiles in Cuba reportedly staff a training base in Cuba where Chilean leftists receive training in guerrilla warfare and terrorist tactics. The trainees are shuttled in and out of Cuba via Buenos Aires and, if caught in Chile, are instructed to say they were trained by Montoneros in Argentina. Meanwhile, Havana has urged the Montoneros in Argentina to work legally within the system.

40. *The America Battalion*. M-19, the Cuban favorite among the several large Colombian insurgent groups, is reportedly not only working to unify the Colombian leftwing opposition (an unlikely proposition) but has also spearheaded the establishment of the America Battalion, a multinational guerrilla force reportedly composed of members of several Latin American insurgent and terrorist groups. Besides M-19, groups reported to be involved include Alfaro Vive, Carajo! of Ecuador, the Revolutionary Movement Tupac Amaru of Peru, and the MIR of Chile—all groups that reportedly receive support and guidance from Cuba. This unit has reportedly been operating in Colombia near the Ecuadoran border.

41. The idea that revolutionaries from several countries should join forces is hardly a new idea in Latin America. It dates from the early 1800s when the Spanish colonies won their independence. More recently:

- In 1974, at the urging of Havana, four South American insurgent groups—the Montoneros of Argentina, the Tupamaros of Uruguay, the MIR of Chile, and the ELN of Bolivia—reportedly joined forces in the Revolutionary Coordinating Junta (RCJ). How real this organization was is debatable, although credit for several terrorist acts was claimed in its name. It has not been heard from since 1977.

- In 1976, again with Cuban encouragement, leftwing extremists in El Salvador, Honduras, Guatemala, and Nicaragua formed the Revolutionary Party of Central American Workers (PRTC), an organization that still exists, on paper, although only the Salvadoran branch is active militarily (it is one—the smallest—of the five components of the FMLN).

42. Whether the America Battalion is really anything more than an M-19 unit with a few foreigners attached remains to be seen. If it is real, whether it will survive the operational setbacks, personality conflicts, disagreements over ideology, goals, and tactics, and other centrifugal forces that cause such organizations to splinter and resplinter also remains to be seen. But if it is real and if it survives, it may develop into a significant adversary in Latin America.

43. In many Latin American countries, the Soviets and Cubans may be supporting local Marxist-Leninists, but they are not at present promoting revolution. In part, this is probably because the governments of these countries do not now appear vulnerable. In addition, though, Havana and Moscow regard some countries—for example, Uruguay, Panama, and Mexico—as hospitable, convenient sites where leftwing insurgents from other countries can meet to plan and coordinate their activities. Reportedly, they regard other countries—Argentina, Bolivia—as valuable staging areas for operations into Chile. Presumably, the Soviets and Cubans understand that the relatively tolerant attitudes of the governments of these countries toward the activities of revolutionaries from other countries would quickly wither if they were beset by leftwing insurgencies of their own.

## The Rest of the Third World

44. *Africa.* Soviet Bloc support of political extremist groups in Africa has diminished in the 1980s, compared with previous decades. In part, that reflects success: rebel groups previously backed by the Soviets in such countries as Angola and Guinea-Bissau are now in power. Indeed, the Soviets now spend more effort assisting counterinsurgency operations in these countries than in promoting Marxist insurgencies elsewhere in Africa—although Soviet military aid to radical South Africans and Namibians doubtless will increase as conditions in southern Africa continue to deteriorate.

45. *African National Congress.* In southern Africa, the Soviet Union and its allies provide the bulk of the weapons and military training received by the African National Congress (ANC). In addition, Moscow strongly influences the South African Communist Party (SACP), whose members in turn strongly influence the ANC's policies and activities by virtue of dominating ANC leadership positions. Most ANC recruits are trained in Angola, sometimes by Cuban and Bloc instructors. Some senior ANC cadre have received training in several East Bloc countries, including the USSR, Bulgaria, and East Germany. The Soviet Bloc also provides the ANC with food, clothing, medicine, weapons, and explosives. Despite its dependence on Communist aid and its numerous Communist leaders, however, the ANC is still better described as a black nationalist organization than a Communist one; moreover, in recent months, ANC leader Oliver Tambo has reportedly been trying to limit Soviet influence over the ANC. And although the Soviets supply the ANC with weapons and explosives, the available evidence does not suggest that Moscow has much input over how they are used.

46. *SWAPO.* Like the ANC, SWAPO has long been dependent on the Soviet Bloc for weapons and military training. The USSR and several of its allies provide a wide range of military equipment suitable for use by conventional infantry units. Equipment destroyed by South African raids on SWAPO's bases in Angola seems to be expeditiously replaced. In addition, Soviet, East German, and Cuban officials furnish SWAPO other forms of assistance, including transport, tactical advice, and training. Troop training is conducted in Angola, but senior cadre have been sent to the Soviet Union, Cuba, and East Germany for training.

47. *Ethiopian Border.* For years, the Marxist regime in Addis Ababa has been involved in proxy conflicts with the Governments of neighboring Sudan and Somalia. Both Sudan and Somalia have supported Ethiopian separatist movements, while Ethiopia—with Soviet Bloc help—has reciprocated by supporting Sudanese and Somali insurgent groups. East German instructors reportedly have helped train both Sudanese and Somali rebels at camps in Ethiopia. Soviet and Cuban instructors reportedly have helped train Somali dissidents at such camps.

48. *Asia.* The Soviet Bloc does not appear to have been involved in most of the terrorism and nonmilitary violence in Asia in recent years. Reported Soviet efforts to establish contact with the New People's Army (NPA) in the Philippines seem to have been halfhearted and ineffectual. Neither the Tamil separatists in Sri Lanka nor the Sikh separatists in India appear to enjoy any Soviet Bloc support. Nor is there any evidence the Soviets are involved with the extreme leftwing groups like Chukaku-ha that occasionally mount terrorist attacks in urban areas of Japan. The story is different, however, in Pakistan.

49. *Al Zulfikar.* Although the Soviet Union generally keeps its distance from pure terrorist groups, it has been directly involved with one such organization—Al Zulfikar, which was founded by the sons and supporters of the ousted and executed former Prime Minister of Pakistan, Zulfikar Ali Bhutto. The Soviets apparently hoped that even if Al Zulfikar proved unable to overthrow General Zia the group might present a threat big enough to make the Pakistanis reduce or cease their support of the Afghan insurgents. In dealing with Al Zulfikar, the Soviets worked through the Afghan intelligence service, which is controlled by the KGB. During the early 1980s, Soviet personnel in Afghanistan reportedly participated directly in training and deploying Al Zulfikar members who were to return to Pakistan to try to destabilize the Zia regime through a campaign of sabotage and subversion.

50. The campaign failed. The group's major terrorist actions, two assassinations and a skyjacking, were highly unpopular in Pakistan, while the skyjackers presented the Soviets and Afghans with a dilemma by taking refuge in Kabul. After the Afghan Government refused to prosecute or extradite the skyjackers, the Summit Seven countries imposed a civil air embargo on Afghanistan (the only time this sanction has ever been implemented). By late 1982 it had become clear that Al Zulfikar was more of an embarrassment than an asset, and the Soviets began disengaging from the group. In response to the declining Soviet support, the members of the group in Kabul moved to Libya and Syria, while other elements of the group reportedly continued to be harbored by India. Since then, the

group has been decimated by a disastrous operational failure in Vienna and the drug-induced death of the younger Bhutto in Paris. During the past two years the group has been inactive. members of Al Zulfikar may have resurfaced in Kabul, which may or may not presage renewed terrorist operations.

51. In addition to manipulating Al Zulfikar, Afghan intelligence agents have mounted a large number of terrorist attacks in the border regions of Pakistan, where Afghan insurgent groups have established safehavens and operational bases. Bombs targeted against cinemas, restaurants, offices, and lodgings have claimed many lives. Afghan Government agents may also be involved in the spread of banditry and kidnapings elsewhere in Pakistan. Soviet advisers are known to assist the Afghan intelligence service in planning its strategy and operations.

## The Developed Countries

52. There is very little evidence of any Soviet or East European involvement with the terrorist groups of Western Europe or other developed countries. Whether they be the nihilist new-left groups—like the RAF in West Germany, the Communist Combatant Cells in Belgium, or Action Directe in France—or the ethnic separatist groups—like the Basque ETA in northern Spain or the Provisional IRA in Northern Ireland—the Soviet Bloc countries seem to keep their distance. Several West European countries—particularly Italy and the United Kingdom—have been able to induce terrorists to confess in exhaustive detail by offering them lenient sentences, and there have been no Soviets in their stories. For its part, the Soviet Union calls such groups "criminal terrorist groups" in distinguishing between them and the "national liberation groups" whose violence it asserts is justified.

53. Since the late 1970s, the USSR has sought to weaken the Western alliance and concomitant support for improvements in NATO strategic and conventional forces by portraying itself as reasonable and peaceable. It has also invested a lot of effort, money, and propaganda in support of the legal left in Western Europe. And it hopes to acquire both technology and investment from West European sources in the coming years. All of this is jeopardized by leftwing extremist violence, which tends to discredit the left in general while pushing frightened moderates toward the right. Finally, the Soviets undoubtedly realize that, with the possible exception of parts of southern Europe, the democratic Western countries are not now vulnerable to leftwing rebellion.

54. *Turkey an Exception*. Notwithstanding the above, there is probably some substance to the numerous reports and allegations of Soviet Bloc involvement with Turkish terrorists over the years. Evidence brought out in connection with the trial of would-be Papal assassin Mehmet Ali Ajca, for example, indicates that the rightwing gangster/terrorist gang known as the Gray Wolves had operated openly in Bulgaria, albeit as gangsters not terrorists. During the 1970s, the KGB reportedly ran a program in Turkey designed to stir up discontent over the US military presence there. Both the leftwing and rightwing extremists who all but fought a civil war in Turkey in the late 1970s got their weapons from Bulgarian sources. After the military regime stifled the prospects of the radical left and reestablished political stability in Turkey, the Soviet Bloc backed off from supporting leftist extremism in that country.

55. Nevertheless, it is evident that the USSR and its East European allies have treated Turkey more like a Third World country than like a part of Western Europe. This case illustrates that, when they have nothing to lose and stand to gain from a change in the status quo, the members of the Soviet Bloc will promote and exacerbate political unrest and violence even in Western Europe, perhaps even when they know the left has no realistic chance of ending up on top.

## Trends and Implications

56. In recent years, although Soviet Bloc efforts to promote Marxist-Leninist revolutions around the world have continued, the overall level of leftwing revolutionary violence has been slowly dropping. This may seem paradoxical, given the rising international concern about it, but consider the following developments of the past decade or two:

— The victory of the Sandinistas in Nicaragua was a notable Communist success, but leftwing revolutionary challenges—some considered very serious at the time—have been beaten back in Portugal, Turkey, Argentina, Brazil, Uruguay, Venezuela, Guatemala, and other countries. Their advances have been slowed or halted in places like El Salvador and Colombia. The number of countries truly threatened by leftwing revolutionaries today is rather low.

— Terrorist assaults in West Germany, Spain, France, Italy, Northern Ireland, and other countries have been stymied or repulsed, and some of the groups involved have been all but obliterated by arrests. True, terrorists still operate in many of these countries, but not at the levels common in the 1970s; and terrorist atrocities still take place in such countries, but not with the frequency of the 1970s.

— As counterterrorist security measures have improved, statistically significant declines have occurred in the number and frequency of airplane hijackings, occupations and barricades of diplomatic facilities, letter bombings, and other formerly common terrorist activities.

— Many international terrorist groups—the Armenian Secret Army for the Liberation of Armenia (ASALA), the PFLP Special Operations Group of Wadi Haddad, the Japanese Red Army, the Carlos Apparat—have been disbanded or become much less active. They have generally not been replaced; only one international terrorist organization—the Abu Nidal Group—now operates on a broad international scale, although new pretenders such as Hizballah bear watching.

57. The halting decline in the fortunes of the violent left has been obscured by developments on the terrorism scene outside the Soviet orbit, including:

— A large and blatant increase in terrorism sponsored by states such as Syria, Libya, and Iran.

— The disintegration of the PLO and the proliferation of small groups of Palestinian terrorist mercenaries whose activities are no longer constrained by a desire to promote the interests of the Palestinian people.

— A major increase in ethnic and religious terrorism on the part of Sikh, Tamil, and especially Shi'ite Muslim extremists.

— The development of Lebanon as a land beyond the law where radical governments and groups have cooperated to create a veritable theme park of terrorism.

58. The increases in Arab, Iranian, Sikh, and Tamil terrorism have little or nothing to do with Communism. Nor does much of the other political violence that occurs around the world. Instead, this violence stems from local and regional disputes of a political, ethnic, or religious nature. Still, in a wider sense, the Soviets do bear some responsibility for the volume of the violence and the readiness with which politically aggrieved groups turn to it. The Marxist-Leninist and Palestinian groups the Sovet Bloc does support have set powerful examples that non-Communists and non-Palestinians consciously emulate, both organizationally and operationally. The Soviet rhetoric that justifies the violent activities of Marxist-Leninists and Palestinians also helps other extremist groups rationalize their violence and makes them less receptive to nonviolent alternatives that might, over time, also alleviate their grievances.

## Outlook

59. The world appears to have reached a roughly steady state of political violence. As guerrilla or terrorist groups in one region are brought under control—or, occasionally, achieve their objectives—guerrillas or terrorists arise somewhere else, in a pattern that almost inevitably will persist. Moscow and its allies will continue to contribute to many of those who choose the violent option.

60. The financial cost of supporting foreign political extremist groups is not significant, compared with the benefits the Soviets evidently feel they receive from such programs. Once committed, moreover, the Soviets and their allies have demonstrated considerable staying power. They are usually patient and reliable supporters, although broader policy considerations may spur change in specific cases—in Zimbabwe, for example, Joshua Nkomo no longer enjoys Soviet backing. In view of the historical durability of these policies, only some major shift in the cost/benefit ratio will lead the Soviets to modify their attitudes and activities in this area.

61. *In the Third World,* Soviet support for insurgent and terrorist groups is seldom encumbered by conflicting policies and goals. If the Soviets wanted to provide more support to such groups—or such support to more groups—there would be little to stop them. Hitherto, they have probably calculated that, at least at first, the added effort would not bring them much besides additional turbulence in the targeted societies. While the Soviets have hardly been opposed to turbulence in non-Communist societies, they have not gone out of their way to create it except in the pursuit of a specific goal (such as the overthrow of the Pinochet regime). A more adventurous approach is conceivable: the Soviets could step up their efforts to disrupt currently stable non-Communist societies in the hope that opportunities for leftist advances would be generated where there are none now. If a moderate govern-

ment were to discredit itself by responding to leftist extremism with not enough skill or too much repression, the Soviets might benefit. We have seen no evidence, however, to suggest that the new Soviet Government is thinking along these lines.

62. *In the Developed World*, where the Soviet Bloc is not known to support groups that engage in political violence, the only substantial change can be in the direction of a greater willingness to do so, either in specific countries or more generally. Considering that their policy of restraint is not principled but only tactical, one of the following developments could conceivably induce the Soviets to change it:

— Serious political instability in a Western country, coupled with improved prospects that the left could come to power there through violence. In the past, during periods of civil turmoil, leftwing extremists in countries such as Portugal, Greece, and Turkey have received Soviet Bloc aid and encouragement.

— An unanticipated opportunity to acquire something of value, such as intelligence, from a West European terrorist group. After the Red Brigades kidnaped US Army General Dozier, the Bulgarian intelligence service, probably at the behest of a Soviet service, tried to arrange through an intermediary to trade weapons and other logistic support in return for any information of military intelligence interest Dozier might have been providing his captors.

— A desire to retaliate against particular Western countries for activities inimical to the interests of the USSR or its allies. Moscow would almost certainly use Third World surrogates. A possible precedent is the probable Soviet sponsorship of the Afghan intelligence service's operations in Pakistan.

63. Neither these nor other external developments that might lead to a change in the Soviet attitude toward providing support for foreign extremists seems likely to materialize, at least not in the short term. It is conceivable, though, that even without any particular stimulus the new Soviet leadership might decide to take a new tack. Nothing in Soviet conduct during the first year of the Gorbachev era suggests this has happened. Throughout the period of the US confrontation with Libya, for example, the Gorbachev regime displayed the same unprincipled, tactical approach toward Libyan terrorism as previous regimes. The Soviet Government apparently made little or no effort to rein in the Libyans, even when provided specific warnings, and it tried to profit as much as possible from the confrontation while not becoming directly involved. Much of its propaganda served to justify Libyan conduct and bolster its reluctance to change that conduct.

64. On the other hand, there have been some changes in the way the Soviets talk about the issue:

— A portion of Gorbachev's speech during the CPSU Congress in February 1986 ("the loathesome face of terrorism") was quoted earlier in this Estimate.

— According to the Soviet news agency TASS, when Qadhafi's deputy, Major Abd al-Salam Jallud, visited Moscow in May 1986, Gorbachev used a statement criticizing the US bombings to admonish the Libyans against provoking the United States further, lest it strike again. Specifically, he cited "the need for adherence to principle and consistency in the condemnation of those pretexts that imperialists use and, first of all, *terrorism in any of its forms*."

— In several official but private forums the Soviets have recently indicated a willingness to discuss ways in which East and West can cooperate to combat transnational terrorism.

65. Whether these indications are anything more than another example of the Gorbachev public relations offensive remains to be seen. If the Soviets are sincere, it will not be difficult for them to demonstrate this in concrete ways. It would be too much to expect, however, that they will ever renounce their "right" to promote Marxist-Leninist revolutions abroad.

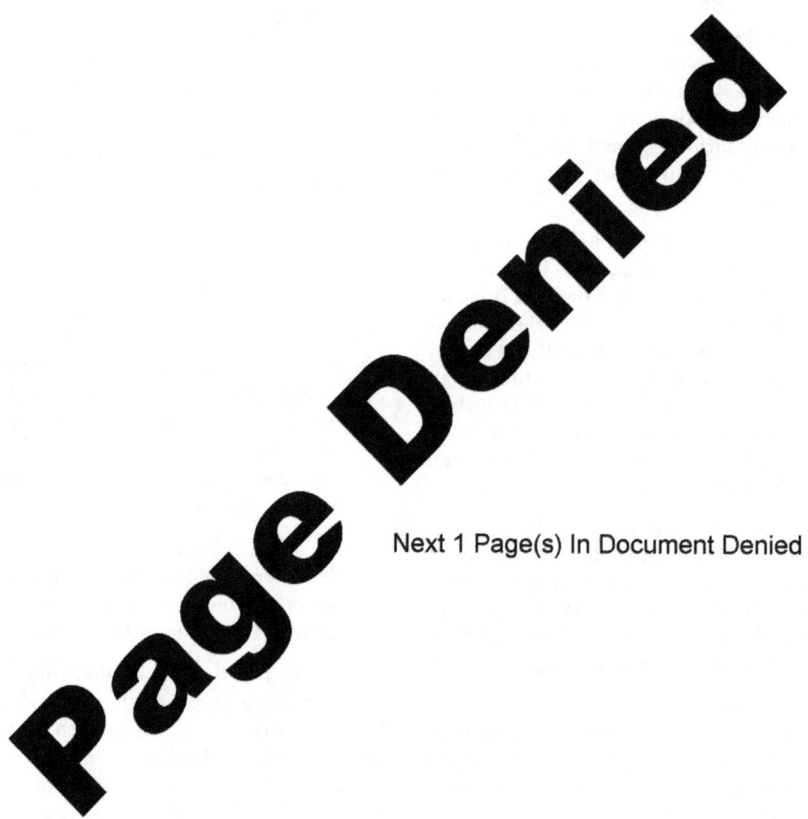